AWAKENING OF
HEART OF THE DEER

HEART OF THE DEER

BALBOA
PRESS

A DIVISION OF HAY HOUSE

Balboa Press books may be ordered through booksellers or by contacting:

Balboa Press
A Division of Hay House
1663 Liberty Drive
Bloomington, IN 47403
www.balboapress.com
1 (877) 407-4847

Because of the dynamic nature of the Internet, any web addresses or links contained in this book may have changed since publication and may no longer be valid. The views expressed in this work are solely those of the author and do not necessarily reflect the views of the publisher, and the publisher hereby disclaims any responsibility for them.

The author of this book does not dispense medical advice or prescribe the use of any technique as a form of treatment for physical, emotional, or medical problems without the advice of a physician, either directly or indirectly. The intent of the author is only to offer information of a general nature to help you in your quest for emotional and spiritual well-being. In the event you use any of the information in this book for yourself, which is your constitutional right, the author and the publisher assume no responsibility for your actions.

Any people depicted in stock imagery provided by Thinkstock are models, and such images are being used for illustrative purposes only. Certain stock imagery © Thinkstock.

Print information available on the last page.

ISBN: 978-1-5043-9623-3 (sc)
ISBN: 978-1-5043-9625-7 (hc)
ISBN: 978-1-5043-9624-0 (e)

Library of Congress Control Number: 2018900967

Balboa Press rev. date: 11/29/2018

DEDICATED TO TRUTH

Acknowledgements

My profound thanks to all my teachers!

To Tommy for encouraging me to write.

To my sons, whose love is unwavering, and all my family members.

To many nameless people simply for being here with me.

To those who are awake: Thank you for standing at the leading edge of life and for the light of love you shine upon the planet.

To the organizations that operate in love's light and are responsible for maintaining and guarding historical records.

Most importantly, to my bestie: the teacher named *Esther.*

PREFACE

Since I started this book I have gone back and forth on whether I should complete it. I have several reasons to withhold my story, but as I examine them, I find their bases are all set in fear, which is not a valid part of my decision-making process. I am therefore forging forward.

I'm sharing this story to provide a perspective on a journey everyone takes. On the surface, our journeys seem different because of our diverse nationalities, families, finances, personalities, and life experiences. But I urge you to look deeper into your life, because it's there that the similarities of our journeys lie.

It's sad that most of us are so enchanted by the lives we are living that we disregard anything outside what we perceive. But I know there are people like you and me who are searching for answers, and it is to these people that I speak.

Our main character's name is Heart of the Deer. This name was given to her as a gift from the Gods. She was told that the deer gives life to the planet, that the deer is alert, graceful, and protective, and that the deer has a warrior heart within. Heart of the Deer is a bright light who brings blessings to the planet. This is the meaning of her name.

She is just learning the truth about the planet. As you read her journey, review your own life, and find the courage to face, thank, and release the difficulties you have endured. Because freedom from the past is another one of my goals. Our past challenges have no place in our future lives unless that is our desire. The ability to release these is the gift I'm giving to myself and offer to you.

It is my sincerest request that God will guide and bless me as I share. I pray that this work will find its way into the hands of my audience and be received in the spirit of love as I intend. It is with humility and appreciation for my unique unfolding that I share this story with you.

Heart of the deer

Prologue

It's an easy night. Everything is quiet, and a gentle breeze glides over my face as I consider the sky. It's the first time in my life that I've really examined this vast dark ocean, and what I see amazes me. It is breathtaking.

At the beginning of my life, I saw the sky as blackness studded with bursts of white, some of them in patterns and others apparently random. My planet's moon is round, but depending on its alignment to the sun, it appears in different phases in the sky. The light from distant stars creates shadows that transform the empty blackness of space into a sea of color and add depth to our perception of it.

Most of my life, I took the night sky for granted. But this year, the picture I see has changed. I now see indigo and cobalt blue, emerald green, ruby red and gold. Sometimes I see a grid like an artist's guide. The first time it happened, I thought I was daydreaming, but now I know the sky is vibrating with energy, and I'm seeing this energy transformed into beautiful colors.

When I gaze into the night sky, I feel overwhelming love and support. It is a pure sensation that brings out goosebumps all over my body even though I'm not cold. I have a smile on my face and warmth in my soul. It is the most satisfied I have ever felt.

The sky is so immense and beautiful that I feel insignificant in comparison. This makes me ask things like, Why are we here? What should I be doing? What is the purpose of my planet in the universe?

I live in the third dimension, in what I call the Learning

galaxy. One of the many planets in this galaxy is called Earth but I think a better name is Mirage. On Mirage, you will find the human family, and that is where my story takes place.

I'm living in the Age of Enlightenment, and I'm in the prime of my life. I knew that the time we live in is often called the Information Age, but I had never heard of the Age of Enlightenment.

My ancestors believed that universal energies influence our planet and its inhabitants. These energies are having a huge impact on my future, but right now I have no idea. If someone were to tell me that, I would laugh at them and think they were delusional. That's because I'm "asleep."

I lived in the northern region of my planet, Freedom Land, in the country called Liberty. I loved all the girly things Freedom Land had to offer even though I often felt they represented vanity and emptiness. I worked in an industry I had never planned to work in, but I flowed naturally from one position to the next and moved up the organizational ladder. Somehow, I had learned to be demanding, selfish, and controlling, which yielded short-term rewards but always left me feeling empty and out of harmony with who I knew myself to be. I longed to return to the loving, kind, joyful, supportive, empathic, carefree girl I remembered.

I knew, instinctively, that the first step to regaining my identity was to remove myself from my marriage, where I had become someone I didn't know or like. This was hard for many reasons: My clan didn't sanction the split. I loved the Almighty and wanted to please him, and my decision ran against my goal of living in harmony with the divine principles my mother and clan leaders had taught me. I desperately wanted to fulfill my covenant with the Almighty and my spouse, but I couldn't command obedience from myself (which in the past I could always rationalize). If I did this, everyone I knew would shun me and my clan would excommunicate me for disobeying the Almighty.

They would think I had turned my back on the Almighty and needed to be punished. My mother would not speak with me, hoping that this would move me to return to the clan and the Almighty's protected flock.

I was in a loving, supportive marriage, and it pained me to hurt my spouse. After all, being loved was what I wanted most. But this love wasn't with the right person, and I knew it was time to leave. I was pained by the hurt I inflicted on my unsuspecting spouse, but I knew it would be better for both of us in the long run.

These consequences broke my spirit, but for some reason I still couldn't make myself obey the Almighty's commandments, so I forged on, apprehensive and alone (which was not unusual, as I always had a deep sense of abandonment), in my quest to regain my identity. It was a time of transition, with infinite possibilities, but all I wanted was to reunite with my best self.

"Heart of the Deer" is my Native Freedom Land name. It was given to me by a sweet woman who said the Almighty had told it to her. She said my name was being changed from Cathy to Heart of the Deer. She said I was a bright light in the world, that the deer gives life to the planet, that the Deer is alert, protective, and graceful and has a warrior heart, and that Heart of the Deer would bring blessings to the planet. She wasn't complementing me, she said: it was the simple truth. This was who I was in my purest form.

But I'm getting ahead of myself. Let's start in my early life.

CHAPTER 1

THE JOURNEY BEGINS

On our planet children are taught to sing this nursery rhyme: *Row, row, row your boat*, gently down the stream. Merrily, merrily, merrily, merrily, life is but a dream. I believe these words were a gift to future generations written under divine inspiration. The cosmos was giving the world two of the keys to unlock life's mysteries.

The intent of the nursery rhyme is to direct attention to the natural current of the planet. The goal is to remind the audience how to navigate this life or at the very least to implant two fundamental messages.

The first message reveals, what is said to be the most powerful invisible law, not only on our planet, but throughout the multiverse. It's an invisible law, which I will compare to gravity; in that we are all subject to. This law provides the transcriber with knowledge and if the knowledge is applied to life, the transcriber will be considered a wise being. Why, because the transcriber will have created a life that follows life's current downstream not fighting for anything, but allowing all desires to manifest. When this is done things miraculously work out and life indeed becomes a merry journey as the nursery rhyme echo's. Desires just materialize, so much so that onlooks marvel at what they (in their ignorance) define as good luck. Like all laws there are positive and negative poles. The negative (only negative in that it is opposite positive) implies going upstream is not natural. The transcriber understands that anyone fighting the current of life (the stream) will meet obstacles at every turn and the journey could be described as many things but merrily; again, supporting the wisdom contained within the nursery rhyme.

The second message contained within the rhyme answers the question why are we here. Simply said we are living within what can be defined as a holodeck. This environment is just a classroom. Spiritual beings (the *us* behind our eyes) come here to grow. But on the way here, we pass through the fountains of amnesia and forget who we are, where we come from, and what we are here to do. This allows for complete acceptance of the life we are born into and we never question its legitimacy that is until we awake.

My earliest memories are now just slides in my brain. Some of them are videos, others are still pictures. But this is my story.

I was born to a beautiful indigenous, strong-willed woman. We lived in Freedom Land. My strongest perception from my early years is that this woman hated me. I mean *hated*, in every sense of the word. Many years would pass before I understood why. In secret, some of my relatives called me a slave, and at night I heard them whispering about how cruel my mother was to me—but how, in the end, I was the one my mother would need the most. They thought I'd be there for my mother even though she wouldn't deserve my help. They'd say, "Poor Cathy." That's my birth name "Heart of the deer" is my Native Freedom Land name and a gift from the Gods.

We were three girls and a boy. I was the middle girl, and my brother was the baby. Whenever my mother introduced us, she proudly says, "These are my little girls," and I noticed that every time the response was the same. People would say to my youngest sister, "Oh my, you are *so beautiful*,"—they emphasized *so beautiful*—and she would thank them. Then they would skip right over me and address my older sister. (I was standing in the middle, but it was like they didn't see me.) They would say to her, "You are so beautiful," and she would thank them. Then they'd turn to me, and in excitement at being acknowledged I'd smile the biggest smile in the world, and they'd hunt for something nice to say and finally settle on "Why, don't you have the prettiest smile," and my heart would sink.

I loved that people thought my sisters were pretty. I could see plainly that they were. But I hoped people would think I was pretty too, but they never said it. So, I began to think I wasn't pretty. I started thinking up excuses. I blamed the hand-me-down clothes I wore, though to be frank they were never all that bad.

This was when I started looking outside myself, to others, for approval. I thought if I was kind to people, they'd like me and might even see the inner me, who I knew was beautiful. Then maybe they'd say I was pretty. But my approach didn't work.

People, especially my mother, just saw me as weak and soft—as someone to exploit.

When both of my sisters got new clothes and I didn't, I asked why. My mother said that my older sister took care of her clothes so they were fine for me to wear, but that after I wore them I ruined them and they were no good for my younger sister. So, it was really my fault that she had to buy new clothes for my youngest sister. I was too clumsy. I suppose it had nothing to do with the quality of the fabric. From this I learned another lesson: that other people deserved more than I did—or, to tell the truth, that my sisters were better than I was. The sooner I accepted that fact, the easier my life would go. So, I accepted it.

One day I was playing with my baby sister, whom I adore. She lit a match, blew it out, and said, "Let's see if it's hot" and placed it on my neck. It burned me, and when I went crying to my mother, she said, "Why are you so stupid, to stand there and let her test it out on you?" But I was too afraid to say I had no idea she was going to test it on me. I was afraid of my mother calling me stupid again so I keep the words in. This is when I learned to stifle my communication.

While learning to wash dishes, I once left the hot water running when I didn't realize the stopper was in place. The sink started overflowing, and I was so afraid of my mother beating me that I mopped up the floor with bath towels. I put the soaked towels in the tub to wash later. Then I dunked my arm into the sink to pull out the stopper. I was burned badly, and my sister had to run out to get my grandfather who lived in a house across the street from our apartment building. He nursed my arm and comforted me, and he asked why I'd knowingly put my arm into scalding water. I told him that my mother would beat me if she saw the sink full of hot water, and I was more afraid of her beating me than of getting burned. He promised to take care of her and that she wouldn't hurt me, and I believed him. As far as I could tell, he was the only person my mother was afraid of. I was happy that he could protect me.

After that I would fantasize about my grandfather beating my mother the way she beat me. I wanted her to get what she'd given. My grandfather was kind to me, but I had heard stories of how he beat his own children for disobedience. I'd even heard that he went to school one day and beat my mother in front of her class. But I figured if he'd done that, she must have deserved it, and I wished he would beat her now because of the way she hurt and humiliated me.

My grandmother never beat her children. She's the kindest woman I've ever met. She was picture-perfect as a grandmother, always loving, hard-working and caring for sixteen children. I thought she didn't belong in this family either—we both got stuck here for some crazy reason. At times, I would sit alone and think something was wrong, and I'd search my mind to figure out how I ended up in such a dysfunctional group. I was so young but knew I didn't belong to this woman.

I loved the kindness my grandparents showed upon me. But it only highlighted the contrast of my mother's cruelty. I couldn't understand how she came out of my grandmother, they were so different.

One day I told my mother I felt sick. She told me to lie down and if I had to vomit to be sure to vomit in the toilet if I needed to. I fell asleep for a while, then woke up suddenly and vomited all over my bed. I started crying because she would kill me for not making it to the bathroom. When she came in, she yelled at me for making a mess, then she threw me in the tub with my sheets and comforter on top of me. She told me to scrub them until they were clean or she would make me eat it. I was crying in the tub as I washed the sheets. I might have been in kindergarten at the time—the sheets were so big I didn't know how I'd finish.

That was a bad night. I felt alone, abandoned and couldn't understand why I'd been born to this woman. That's a question that has stayed with me. Now, of course, I'm grateful to her simply because she provided me with a strong contrast to love. Because of her example, I made it my goal to be kind. I could have learned the same lesson from a loving mother, I know, but I make the best out of what life gives me, and the contrast this woman provided awakened a strong desire in me to be loving.

My mother had several brothers, and one of them really liked me. His name was Harold. We'd play this game whenever he visited. He'd chase me around, and when he caught me he'd tickle me till I couldn't breathe. He'd say, "Stop laughing! Stop laughing!" but of course I couldn't, and when I lost my breath he would take me to the bathroom, hang me upside-down over the toilet, and say, "Ok, this is your last chance! You need to control yourself, or I'm going to flush you down the toilet!"

I would scream and hold on to him for dear life. Maybe it sounds a bit disturbing to you, but this was the most fun I had as a child. There were a few good times then, and I am thankful for them.

I learned to clean from a type-A personality: my mother. She taught me to fold sheets without help and to make a bed with hospital corners even before I started school. She would inspect my room after I cleaned, and if she found one thing out of place I had to start all over. She'd look through the dresser, and if one thing wasn't folded right she would pull out every drawer, dump the clothes in a heap, and make me start again. If the bed wasn't made perfectly—if there was a wrinkle, if the corners weren't tight enough—she'd pull the sheets off and I'd have to start from scratch. So, as you can imagine, I was sheepish whenever I reported that my room was clean.

Without intending to, we started playing a sort of game. When she was busy she'd ask, "Are you sure you want me to check your room?" these words gave me butterflies in my stomach. I'd say, "Let me just check one thing," and I'd go back and inspect my room again. When I finally thought, everything was in perfect order, I'd muster up the courage to tell her I was ready again. Without fail, she would find something I had missed. It was as if from her height see could see things better than I could. I dreaded this process. The lesson I learned was that I had to be perfect or I would be found out, exposed. I also learned to pay attention to the small things and that my best could always be improved on.

My mother said the floor should be clean enough to eat off, and that took constant cleaning. She was obsessed with cleanliness, and it had to be my obsession too, but all wanted to do was be a child and play.

When I was in first grade, my teachers told my mother that I was gifted and they wanted to skip me ahead a grade. She told me this, but said she would take care of it—she said I wasn't smart enough to complete the grade I was in, let alone be moved ahead. The next day she went to the school and told them that I just had a good memory but didn't understand things, and that they had to hold me back, not push me forward. So, I was forced to repeat the first grade instead. After that, I never tried hard at school. I just did the bare minimum in order to pass. Later on, my older sister was skipped a grade, and I didn't understand why it was ok for her but not me. I guess I was right: she really was better than me.

I haven't really talked about the beatings. They were so frequent that *not* being beaten was the unusual thing, for me. My mother just hated me, and nothing I did pleased her. She was cruel, and I was sure I deserved better. I would look at her from time to time and wonder, *who are you and why do I live with you?* Even at that age I recognized I was different than she was. I thought, *I'm kind and you are not. You are evil, but something inside of me is bigger than you and I will not let you break my will. One day you'll see how good I am, and I hope then you'll finally be able to acknowledge my importance.* What I didn't understand was that she was a young energy and still learning to deal with life's contrasts.

Wouldn't it be ironic to learn after death we had lived many lives and before my mother's birth I agreed to help this being grow and that she agreed to help me grow to learn love? But then when we were born our discussions were forgotten and yet somehow, we lived out our intentions? Wouldn't it be crazy if the same was true of you? My ancestors say this is the case- I have no way of verifying these statements, but they are seeds for thoughts, aren't they?

When my mother spoke with her friends and family, they would talk about the Holy Texts or about how pretty they looked and how they could get any men they wanted. They'd talk about controlling men and about how powerful they were, but I didn't agree with them. They didn't seem powerful in their marriages. My mother and father fought. He would really beat her, and she'd fight back like a man in the streets, but he was just stronger. Afterward, she would have one of her brothers come over and beat my father for hitting her, and she would cheer her brothers on like we were at the Colosseum. One time another one of my Uncles, who I never really knew much about, was beating up my father in front of our building, and my mother made me watch through the window. We lived on the third or fourth floor, and she cheered for her brother from the apartment window. My father was bleeding, but he wouldn't give up, so he just kept getting beaten. In the end, my grandmother had to go into the street and pull my uncle off. It was a terrible thing to witness. Even though I never felt anything for my father, even though he was more a stranger than a relative, I didn't like seeing anyone get hurt like that.

My mother always bragged that if anyone tried to hurt her, she would kill them, and if she couldn't one of her brothers would. I wondered, *How can you be married to someone and claim to love them, but fight with them and want them to get beaten up?* I asked her this once, and she said that he had tried to hurt her so he deserved it. She said he was stupid because he got beaten down every time they fought: "Here he thinks he's hurting me she said, but he's really just hurting himself." The way I saw it though, she was stupid for staying with someone who would beat her. *If he deserves to be beaten up for hitting on you, what do you deserve for beating me I thought, but I didn't say a word?* As soon as I was old enough, I decided, I would leave her. I didn't belong in this family and couldn't understand how I'd been born into it. They were barbaric. Sometimes I daydreamed that a birth worker had given me to the wrong family, and that one day my real parents would find me, and rescue, and love me.

That never happened. But somehow, maybe because I had great grandparents and other good relatives, I survived.

One night I awoke to shouting and went to find out what was happening. I arrived in time to see my mother hurl a large glass vase down the hallway, just missing my father as he ran out the door. When I looked back at her, I saw that she was crying, I instantly felt sorry for her. My heart jumped out of my chest and I wanted to protect her, but it was all over. That night was when I learned that she really had feelings just like mine, and that she was human like me. But when I asked her if she was ok, she just told me clean up the mess and went into her room. I put shoes on because broken glass was everywhere. I cleaned up carefully and thought about how crazy she was. I mean, who would lose a fight and then start breaking things they loved, pretty things? I resolved never to fight like those people. And if I somehow found myself in a fight, I wouldn't break my own things and be stuck cleaning up the mess, another life lesson.

When I was in second grade, we moved into a new neighborhood. Before we went into the market, my mother told me I'd see children asking for things and their mothers telling them no, and then these kids would fall on the ground throwing tantrums, screaming and crying. She told me that if

I tried that, she'd step on my chest and crush me. I knew she meant it. I didn't even know why she told me the story—I was already too afraid to imagine behaving like that.

But I do remember one day clearly. My mother was yelling at me for no reason, just being a bully, and I was thinking about how sick I was of her hitting me. When she grabbed me by the shoulders and started shaking me, something snapped in my head. I said, "That's enough. I've had it with you always hurting me!" and then I pulled my arm back and slapped her as hard as I could. I was only in second grade—it wasn't hard enough. I remember her smiling at first, and then saying, "Oh, you think you are grown? You think you can hit me? Well know this, little one. If you're big enough to hit, then you're big enough to get hit back." And then she beat the crap out of me.

It hurt, and I was crying, but I was thinking, *You mean that now you'll use this as an excuse to beat me. Well, what excuse did you have for beating me all these years when I never hit you? Did you think I was grown up then? The only difference is that now you're sitting on me too. Let's face it—you never needed a reason.*

I was hurt physically, but emotionally I felt powerful. For the first time, I had stood up for myself. I learned a few lessons that day. I learned never to raise my hand to her. I learned that people didn't need reasons for what they did. People would do what they wanted, but if I gave them a reason it would be easier, so I should never give them ammunition. I also learned that I believed no one had the right to hit me, and that I could stand up to Goliath. I learned that I had strength inside me. I learned courage.

My mother held weekly Holy Texts studies with us. She wanted us to remember the fruitage of the Almighty's spirit. She assigned different fruitages to each of us. I was joy and goodness, which I fully embraced—I thought, *For once she's getting something right.*

I have a light complexion, and my bruises from beatings were very apparent. My mother would dress me in thick tights with long-sleeved blouses and sweaters and warn me not to show anyone my bruises. She said if I did, I'd be taken away, and my life would be terrible because the authorities would put me in foster care. In foster care, she said, little girls were sexually abused, and no one would ever adopt me because humans who adopted children only wanted infants. So, I was very careful to conceal my bruises at school. I was so afraid of going somewhere worse.

My mother also complained that I was too skinny. She gave me pills called Weight-On, but thank the Almighty, they didn't work. And she didn't like how light my skin was, so in the summer she made me stand in the sun to get darker. She kept my sisters in the shade because she liked their skin color.

By time I turned 10 the consistent beating stopped. My mother was distracted with working and living her life. I had also learned to stay out of her way. When she was home you could find me in a room far away from her.

It was only years later that I learned that my mother had been raped, and that's how I was conceived. She was yelling at me and just blurted it out, right in front of my high school boyfriend: "You always ruin everything! I've never loved you.

13

You've been a burden for me, and I want you to know I hate you. Your father raped me, and I was stuck with a child I never wanted. When you have children, you'll see that they have the mannerisms of their parents. I watched you grow, and I never understood you. You were foreign to me, and I just wanted you dead. I tried so many times to kill you before you were born. So, let's be clear—I don't love you and I don't want anything to do with you. Whenever I look at you, you remind me of your father and his brutality."

I was in shock. What can you say when your mother tells you she hates you and wishes you were dead?

With all the abuse, I suffered, I can't believe that I love my mother as much as I do. I think she was crazy and mean, of course, but I feel sorry for her too, and I thank her for the many life lessons I learned.

If this life is just a dream, my biggest lesson in it has been one of love. My mother was the opposite of love, and as I said, I was determined to be different than her. I made it my goal to be loving toward people (which I don't always achieve but at least I try), and I owe this to the woman who abused me.

I guess things work out in the end. My aunts were right— my love for her is unconditional, and I will be there for the woman whose smile I see in the mirror. I'll be there for the woman whose body nourished my developing cells in her womb. I'll be there for the woman who loved as deeply as she hated me. She's passionate, and at her core she is good. More of her core has showed as the years have gone on. She's softened, and I think she would be enjoying life now—but she still needs to learn the most important lesson. She must learn to *forgive herself.* She carries a heavy load compounded of the burdens of all her past mistakes, and she is causing herself much pain and sickness. This is one of the reasons I'm making it my goal to face the abuse and the false lessons. I've learned to thank life and the difficult experiences because they have always worked out for my highest good and then to release them. I'm wanting to release the stress they implanted within my body which will allow for my healing. I strongly encourage you to do the same.

I wish my mother peace and I thank her for being clean, for caring for my daily physical needs, and for teaching me hard work.

I thank her for protecting me from the dark side of this world, even if she couldn't protect me from herself. I thank her for never using addictive drugs to escape reality, I thank her for not aborting me. Thanks for life, Mom. I thank her for many things, but most of all I thank her for teaching me to love.

Row, row, row your boat, gently down the stream, Merrily, merrily, merrily, merrily, life is but a dream. The nursery rhyme is a reminder of the invisible laws of our planet and the dream state we are in. So, I cannot hold resentment toward my mother because she could not permanently hurt me—after all, I'm dreaming. And the truth is, so are you. But you must wake up to realize it.

Chapter 2

Be Careful What You Wish For: Thirty-Five Years Later

I'd been invited to a fundraiser. I didn't give much thought to what I'd wear, though, when Saturday arrived I found myself standing in the middle of my massive closet, completely at a loss. In the end, I settled on a black, floor-length silk evening dress with a scooped neck and a long-slit running halfway up my thigh. I added pearl earrings, black pumps, a beaded clutch, and bound my long black hair up in a bun to complete the look.

My husband, Still Waters, knew I was readying myself to go somewhere, but he didn't inquire. He'd been wandering around the house acting like a lost puppy, ever since I told him I wanted a divorce. I felt sorry, but I set myself on guard against emotional manipulation. More times than I could count he'd acted sad about something or other, and I'd felt badly and given in. But not this time. I didn't mean to hurt him. I just wanted out. I needed to be free of him. My thoughts drifted back to how I'd ended up here.

I married him because I wanted to be a good, spiritual woman. I'd dated my share of other men, but now I was going to follow the holy books and look at the spiritual qualities of a man. This time I wanted to know if he loved the Almighty and feared displeasing him. Was he intelligent, kind, hard-working, family-oriented, independent and a man who not only came home each night but who engaged with the household.

I had a list, but I didn't need a prophet, just a good guy. My rule was, if the man had eighty percent of what I wanted, I'd let the other twenty percent go. After all, I might only be eighty percent of what someone else wanted. I thought I was being realistic.

So, I was willing to overlook twenty percent, as long as that twenty percent didn't fall into my *Hell no, no way* category.

That category was reserved for what I referred to as bad guys: men who beat women, cheaters and womanizers.

I met Still Waters through a friend in the clan. He seemed like a good being, and he had eighty percent of what I wanted. From what I could tell, we had the same beliefs, and this was the most important thing to me. He was also very intelligent, kind, hard-working, and family-oriented, and we liked many of the same things. He accepted me as I was, and that felt good. He didn't treat me as a possession. He treated me as a partner. He loved me and I felt I owed it to him to return that love.

The twenty percent he was missing had to do with looks, how he dressed, the lack of swagger and security. I didn't want anyone arrogant, of course, but he was short on self-confidence, the kind you show non-verbally. I don't mean to imply that he was modest because —he wasn't- he knew he was smarter than most, and he used that in place of self-confidence. There was an edgy forcefulness to him when he acted this way, it was as if he was daring those he met nonverbally, conveying Bring it on. I'll mentally whip you and I'll put you in your place. Add extreme introversion to it, and you end up with a being who projects a persona of aloofness. These were certainly not endearing traits.

But he also had the sweetest smile and the kindest eyes, and I loved his even temperament. I liked what I saw behind his eyes. There was depth there, intelligence, gentleness and generosity. I liked the shape of his nose (very independent), his mouth (not too big or small), and the sound of his voice (smooth, with excellent diction), and he had beautiful skin. He was an introvert who studied the patterns around him, and I was a solid, middle-ground extrovert who saw the world in black and white. Needless to say, I didn't always understand how he processed information, but I worked hard to comprehend him. He taught me a lot about our sacred books.

He put me first, and that felt good. We had finally reached the point where we were relaxed and growing together.

We dated with chaperones, as the tribe demanded, so we weren't intimate before our marriage. The problem was, I wasn't a virgin. I already had good sex.

On our honeymoon, I discovered he suffered from PE (premature ejaculation). He tried to please me in other ways, but that was even worse. And he had a body odor in his private area that was so strong I thought I'd throw up when I first smelled it. He said that no matter how he tried, he couldn't get rid of it. I thought, *Seriously!* The whole situation was just horrible.

The Almighty has a strange sense of humor, but I wasn't laughing. I almost left Still Waters that night, but his eyes were so sad that I just couldn't bring myself to. Instead, I waited till we got home and called a tribe leader. I said there were some problems, without describing the details as I didn't want to betray Still Waters confidence. But it turned out I couldn't leave, not unless he broke the covenant by having intimate relations with another. I said, Well I'm leaving anyway. And the tribe leader said, Heart of the Deer, listen carefully: *you will stay married or be excommunicated from the Almighty*. I couldn't imagine living without the Almighty's favor. I hung up the phone and cried for two days.

So, I stayed married, and I made the best I could of it for more than a decade. What I learned over that decade was to swallow my own desires. As a result, I started turning into someone I didn't know and didn't like.

Still Waters asked, suddenly, Are you ok? You're just standing there. His voice snapped me back to reality. And when I saw his face, I heard myself blurt out an invitation to join me. I'm ok, I added, I was just daydreaming I guess.

I still loved him and enjoyed his company, of course, I just didn't want to be married to him. But it was the tone of his reply that pierced my heart. He said, Why would I want to go with you when you're not interested in me, and you want a divorce? *No*, I don't want to go anywhere with you.

It pained me to hear this. Of course, I was interested in him. Wasn't it me who took care of him when he was sick? Didn't I hold his hand through life's disappointments? Hadn't I played the bad guy so that he could be the good guy and save face in tough family situations? Didn't I deal with his inability to satisfy me? Hadn't I been his full-on cheerleader for over a decade? Of course, we still enjoyed each other's company, and of course we'd be kind to one another, because we were kind people.

What was he saying? I wondered. But I didn't ask. Instead I thought, I've hurt him and the only words that will take away his pain are the ones I won't say: *I'll stay. We can fix this.* Instead I said, Suit yourself, just thought I'd ask, thought you'd want to get out of the house.

With those words still lingering in the air, I went to the garage, got into my car, and left. As I drove off I took in the backdrop in my mirror.

Thirty minutes later I pulled up at my colleague Vanessa's house. She ran out to greet me and said, You park, I'll drive. She wore a trendy outfit that fit amazingly with her razor-short pixie haircut and flawless makeup.

The temperature was perfect. I've always loved September nights because September seems like the month that delivers the planet from the long hot days of summer. Now the days were shorter and the earth was cool. The air was clear and smelled of new-cut grass. I looked out at the majestic mountains and thanked the Almighty for all the goodness I enjoyed. This planet is so beautiful.

We pulled up and the valets opened our doors. Inside the hotel, an attendant greeted us and showed us to the ballroom and our table. At once a waiter appeared and took drink orders. I took club soda—I don't like the taste of alcohol—and Vanessa took wine. We scanned the room for familiar faces, but decided to save the mingling for later and focus on our own table.

Across from me sat the president of a marketing company, who'd clearly had too much to drink. His skin was bright pink, and broken capillaries which made a sort of jigsaw puzzle on his skin. His hands were swollen like the hands I'd seen on humans with gout— `his wedding ring was so tight, I wondered how blood could flow past it. But he was a jolly fellow, too. He told us stories about his summer vacation and an event he'd just attended for the governor. His silver hair had just enough black left to signal his fading youth. Why was it, I wondered, that men of his age always seemed to have the same bellies as women seven months pregnant? I shook my head.

His wife was all of twenty-five, with full lips and large breasts. Need I say more? She drank too much too, but instead of being jolly she was embarrassing. She bubbled with over-the-top with happiness and was too loud for my taste. She was locked in conversation with a plain-Jane senior to her left, who had just retired from teaching.

The husband, I think his name was Paul, was going on about how they'd spent July at the vineyard and all of June traveling Europe. He said he was the official luggage carrier, and basically satisfied her every wish during their trips. She interrupted to say that it was how he made up for being so busy during the year— she couldn't *count* all the business trips and late nights his work demanded. Honestly, she said, it's like I'm a single lady for ten months out of the year.

Then she turned her pretty young face toward his and said, But boy, does he do a great job making it up to me.

The retired teacher chimed in to point out how great it was having eight weeks off every summer, even if she couldn't live as extravagantly and they did. She talked about now having time for painting and other things she loved. Then she paused, and added, But now every day's a vacation when you're retired. She turned her lips up to form a gentle smile.

A surgeon and his wife was also sitting with us. They had four children who were away attending college. He was a big guy in a black suit and tie, with large eyes and a deep tan. Her skin was a dark chocolate color, and she looked vibrant and healthy— she wore almost no makeup, and few accessories beyond her beautiful smile.

The time came for me to excuse myself and look at the items up for bidding. As I perused the displays, I noticed a tall, thin man making his way around the room, greeting people with a big smile. He seemed to know everyone. His head was bald, almost shiny over his rich black suit, and as he passed I saw that his eyes were crystal green. He looked a bit old, but he moved confidently and happily.

I put my name on some items of interest and then set out to do a little mingling. I ran into a casual acquaintance, but Randy seemed to get nervous when I walked up, and acted as if he didn't know me. His wife was nowhere around for me to speak to. I didn't know what that was all about because I knew both of them, but instead of reminding him, I gave up and went to the bar for another drink. There I ran into a drunkenly rude older man. It saddened me a little, the way alcohol brought out the worst in some people, but I shook it off and moved on. Eventually I had good chats with people I knew and was introduced by them to others.

After the auction, there was music and dancing. It didn't take much coercing from Vanessa to get me up. We danced for a few songs, and when I sat down again Vanessa asked a guy nearby to join her. He looked sheepishly at his wife and said,

I'm married. This is what I love about Vanessa: she just turned to his wife and said, Let's all dance. And so, they did.

As I sat listening to the music and watching the people let loose, the bald man in the black suit came up and introduced himself. He said, Hi, I'm Cain, and extended his hand. I said, Hello, My name is Heart of the deer. His hand was smooth and soft but I felt strength in them too, a nice combination. He asked if he could join me, and I said sure. He sat down and asked, Where are you from? I said I was from Freedom land. He asked what had brought me to Independence City, and I said I'd gotten married, so my husband had.

Abruptly, he said, I'm very sorry, but would you please excuse me for a moment?

I said, Of course, and watched as he followed another woman, who was leaving.

How rude, I thought, and turned back to the dance floor. Vanessa was just arriving at the table. She asked, What that guy's name? I'm jealous— you know I love tall, light-eyed men. Beautiful ones especially.

I laughed and said I would introduce her if we met again.

She replied, Oh no you won't! I'm not taking your leftovers! I've got another man on my mind tonight. He had plans earlier, but he just texted me and said he's free now. A bunch of us are going to a dance club after this is over, and you should join us.

I had ridden with Vanessa so I was happy to go. We danced some more, and this time Randy came up to me and said hi and talked for a few minutes. I thought, *Oh, you remember who I am now, and you want my attention.* It was strange.

Eventually I said my goodbyes and excused myself to the ladies' room. The club soda was running straight through me. As I was washing my hands, Vanessa found me: Oh great, there you are. Let's go, I need to pick up Michael.

Cain was standing right outside the restroom as we exited. Vanessa grabbed his hand and said, There you are. Let's go, we're going dancing. Cain walked beside us with a smile. When the valet brought Vanessa's car she said to me—right in front of Cain—You ride with him so Michael can ride with me. Just follow me.

I was surprised— we didn't even know this man— but went along with it. I asked Cain, Is this ok with you? My car is at her house. He said, Absolutely. So, we set off.

I don't know what made me say this, but I just blurted out, You've spent a lot of time with older women in your family. There are a lot of women that are close to you and very important in your life, and you love the holy wittings, and so do I.

Upon hearing my words, he smiled and said, Yes, I come from a large family. I have several sisters I'm really close to, and my grandfather was a spiritual leader. What's your favorite book in the cannon of holy writings?

Esther, I said. He asked why, and I said that when I was a child, I was determined to have my favorite book be named after a woman. Which limited my options, then I chuckled. When I grew up, I said, I learned that Esther lived with her uncle, and I wondered what happened to her parents and felt sad for her. I loved the wisdom and courage she showed in saving her nation—really, she risked her life to expose the bad guy and defend her people— she won my respect and heart.

He smiled and said, I love Esther too, but because it's my mother's name. He asked how I knew about his family and I said, I don't know, I just sometimes know random things for no reason. I can read your handwriting too, I said.

He said, Oh yeah? We'll see.

I smiled and turned to face the window. As he drove, I got lost in the scenery of the night. After a while, he said, So tell me about your husband. You said you moved here to get married.

I told him it was a long story, but we were getting divorced. I said, I'm moving out soon. I just need to find a place. I was living in a 5 thousand square feet home on 5 acres of land at the time. I couldn't decide if I wanted a big place or a small, cozy one. What I wanted, I told him, was the best place to start this new chapter of my life. I was going make a decision that week and move out by the end of the month. He smiled as he pulled into a gas station behind Vanessa.

We waited as she pulled up to another car, and the driver got out of his own car and into hers. She pulled out again, and we were soon back on the highway. Cain said, Oh I know where she's going. She just didn't take the direct route. He turned on the radio and asked, Do you like jazz? I said yes. I love almost all music.

With jazz playing in the background, I asked what the deal was with him running after that lady earlier. Not that I cared, I'd just thought it was awkward not to mention rude.

He said, Oh, she's an old friend, and I didn't want her to walk to her car alone.

I wondered why didn't she use the valets, then thought what a gentleman he was, and then figured there must be more to the story, but it didn't really matter.

As he parked I said, Since you drove, I'll pay the cover fee. He showed his white teeth. He had a beautiful smile that drew you in.

Inside the club, I had him write his name on a napkin. I folded it and put it in my purse to review with him later. We danced through the night and into the early morning, and before we knew it the club was closing.

Vanessa suggested we go get breakfast. There weren't many options at 2 a.m., so we all knew the place she had in mind. Cain said, We'll see you there.

We arrived first and took a table for four. While we waited, I pulled out the napkin and studied Cain's signature. I said, ok I'm ready.

What do you think? he asked.

Well first, I said, this might not always be the case, because our handwriting changes with our moods. And you didn't write enough for me to do an in-depth analysis. But here's what it says. It says you are very independent, and passionate, and set in your ways. It says you want to be in a relationship— you don't like being alone.

I looked up and smiled. How did I do?

He said, There's only one correction I'd make. I do like being alone sometimes.

When the others arrived, Vanessa sat across from me, and we ordered food. When it arrived, I knew at a glance that I wouldn't like mine. But Cain's French toast looked delicious. I must have been too obvious, because he took one look at my face and said, Why don't we share? I quickly agreed.

He started cutting the French toast into small squares and dousing them with syrup. Then he cut the strawberries and bananas into matching sizes.

I expected him to put some on my plate, but instead he lifted a forkful to my mouth, so I opened, still a little surprised, and he gently placed it inside. When I closed my mouth, the sweetness of the syrup and the tartness of the strawberries brought my taste buds to life.

Then Vanessa said in disgust, Are you kidding me? I'm stuck with this guy, and that's what you get?

Her words caught us off guard, but her date didn't seem to mind. He did seem crazy about her, but she didn't seem interested in him anymore. Something must have happened between them— she'd been so excited earlier.

After we paid she said, Let's go back to my house and salvage this evening. Cain and I were in, so again we found ourselves following her down the highway. When we arrived, the guard recorded our license plate and opened the gate to let us into the community. We parked at Vanessa's house and went in. She had already put music on and brought out drinks. Cain and I sat on the couch and talked. He asked me about all sorts of subjects, I shared feely and felt right at home. After a while, Vanessa's conversation with her friend moved into the next room. When a song came on that Cain and I both liked, we sat back and I leaned my head against his shoulder. He placed his head upon my head, and we fell fast asleep.

It was a pain in my neck that woke me. The clock said it was four in the morning. Vanessa and Michael were not around. I nudged Cain and told him, I'm going to lie down in one of the guest rooms. Feel free to use one, or you can just stay here.

He said, May I lie down with you? I promise I'll be on my best behavior. I said that would be fine, as long as the clothes stayed on. So, for the first time in more than a decade, I found myself sleeping in the arms of a stranger. Years later, he told me that we had spooned that night.

I'd never heard the expression.

Cain woke me a couple hours later and said, I have to go home and cook my daughter breakfast. It's a Sunday tradition.

I said great, and as I closed the front door, Vanessa called out to ask, Is he leaving?

I said yes, and she said, Please go get him and have him take Michael to his car.

I opened the front door and motioned Cain back to ask him. As the two men drove off, Vanessa said, Thank the Almighty Michael's gone. I don't want to see him again. So how was the sex?

I ignored her question and asked what had happened: You were crazy about him, then you didn't seem to like him at all, I said.

She said, He likes me too much, and he has young kids. He's not what I'm looking for long-term.

I said, Oh— was he disappointed when you told him?

She waved the question away: I didn't tell him I won't talk to him again.

Well, what did you guys talk about?

She laughed. Who said we talked? I couldn't wait for him to leave, but I didn't want to be rude. When I heard you and Cain moving around, I jumped up and thought, *Please get this man out of here.*

Then she laughed again. I really liked Vanessa, she was a lot of fun, but I didn't understand how she could share her body so casually. But oh, well. No judgements from me.

Vanessa filled a cup with coffee and turned back to me: So, tell me, how was the sex?

I said I didn't have sex, and she said, Stop lying, girl. I don't care.

I said, No, honestly, we fell on asleep on the couch.

I woke up with a pain in my neck and told him I was going to the bedroom, and he asked if he could go with me if he behaved. We went into the guest room and slept. We even left the door open.

She shook her head and said, You're so boring.

I said, No, girl, I'm careful.

As I drove home, I thought about the previous evening and how it was that I so easily spent time with another man while I was still married. To my surprise, I didn't feel guilty about my night. I wasn't divorced yet, but in my mind, I guess we already were. I told myself it was completely PG13, though Still Water would be crushed if I told him. I'm sure the very sight of me would disgust him and I couldn't hold that against him, he'd be right, my behavior was unacceptable and lacked dignity. He might act as Vanessa had, disbelieving my story that nothing improper happened. I decided I would only tell him if he asked and I decided not to beat myself up over it. I was sorry but I'm not going to say I didn't enjoy the attention from Cain because that would be a lie. I thought if Still Waters had come along, it would have gone very differently, but it wasn't his job to manage my behavior, that was my responsibility and I love it that way. I knew what I did was wrong but I reasoned I'll be divorced soon. Still Water never asked and so I didn't share.

Cain called a few days later and invited me to dinner. I was with Vanessa at the time, and said I already had plans but would love a raincheck. I got one a few days later. Vanessa joined us this time, but Cain distracted her by calling his brother and letting them speak. He held my hand during dinner and kissed me a few times on my hands and once on my face. It was all really sweet, but Vanessa said, Just get on with already, and we all laughed. We went on this way for a couple of weeks, and I was liking him more with each date.

A week before my birthday, I found a new place. It was small but perfect, and I was happy. I invited Cain over to check it out before my furniture was delivered. I was excited about my new start, and as we toured my home Cain said, I'm really proud of you for getting a smaller place. You don't need a lot of space for one person.

I said, You're right. But let's see how I adjust. My furniture took eight weeks to be delivered, so whenever Cain came over we sat in a bay window or on the barstools. I loved how comfortable he was, and it was really cool of him to hang out there when there was no furniture. I acted like I was in college. We enjoyed being together like two kids who didn't have much. It was all about us, not the material things.

It was here in my new place, after the furniture was delivered, that we had our first sexual encounter. He kissed me on the mouth, gently, and moved toward my ear and down my neck, which tickled at the slightest touch. Did I mention that he had big hands? With one swift movement, he picked me up in them and carried me to my bed. Then he said, Let me give you a full body massage and spend the night pleasuring you.

I smiled. I said, If share myself with anyone, it means a lot to me. The holy writings say fornication is the only sin that happens in our bodies. All the other sins happen outside. It was crazy that I only focused on that part of the text, but was fully willing to commit fornication—or better said, adultery, as my divorce wasn't yet final. I don't know what I was thinking, but I continued: I want it to be meaningful and limited to one person. If you can commit yourself to me, then yes.

Without hesitation, he said, Didn't I tell you I'm a one-woman man? It's easy for me to honor that stipulation. He kissed my forehead and said, I'm here with you and only for you.

Then he stood me up and slowly, tenderly undressed me and laid me on my stomach. He lit a white candle that stood on the dresser and took oil bottles, hand towels, and a white cotton robe from his bag. I thought, *Oh, you've been planning for this. I wondered how long his bag had been packed?* He took his

33

clothes off too, and put on the robe, being careful not to show me his body. He set the oils on the nightstand and said, Close your eyes and relax.

First, he moved my long hair off my back and onto the pillow beside my head. Then soaked his warm strong hands with oil that smelled of lavender, and ran them down my spine, then back up and out toward my shoulder blades, and up and around my shoulders and the crook of my neck. He moved in, up, back, down, and out, making just the slightest adjustments with each pass. My back felt like a piece of dough being kneaded lovingly by a baker.

He moved his hands back into my spine and worked down into my lower back and my waist, then down to my buttocks, thighs, calves, and even my feet. He massaged out every kink I had. It was clear he was making a mental roadmap, of what my body loved. And just when I couldn't take another moment of it, he turned me over and did the same on my front side. As he worked my inner thighs, he kissed my stomach, and then my breasts, giving every part of my body generous attention. He'd already caused me to lubricate naturally, but when he worked on my breasts the moisture between my legs began to overflow. We made love into the early morning hours. It was this exchange that I longed for during my marriage to Still Water, but we were never able to create it. Now over a decade later I found myself enjoying one of the most intimate connection two beings can make and I did it outside of marriage.

As I laid on his chest He said, I've been wondering for a

while what it would be like to be with you like this. And I must say, you surprised me in a good way.

I asked, How did I surprise you? and he said, By letting go and going with it. I thought for sure you'd object to some of it, but I was glad you let go. It made the experience more fluid, and I hope more enjoyable for you.

I said, I savored every second we were together. And, you're right, I'm new to a few of your tricks. I almost stopped you when you were putting the oil on me. I thought you were going to do something different, but I'm thankful you didn't.

No other lover ever shared all of themselves with me like he did. I loved the exchange, I loved his smell, his kisses, his strength and his tenderness. I guess he had me wide open, hooked like a drug user. Experiences like these are etched forever into my mind.

The next day as I sat on my couch I thought about my life. I wished for freedom from Still Water, and I got it (as my divorce would be finalized in a couple days). I wished for the love Still Water gave me, but from someone else, someone made for me. Was Cain the answer to my wish?

I wished to be free to live my life the way I wanted, without having to conform to my tribe, my mother, my family and my friends, and now I'm free of them.

As I look back over my life, I must ask myself whether I really got what I wished for, or whether I should have heeded the warning from my ancestors: ***Be careful what you wish for,***

You just might get it. Would this warning be part of my growth or had I interpreted and navigated the terrain wisely? Was it independence and bliss that caused my awaking, or something else? You tell me . . .

CHAPTER 3

PANDORA

Cain and I dated for two years before I moved in with him. We lived together for another year before marrying. We never fought, and only once had he used cruel words with me. I reasoned that anyone could have a bad day, so I didn't pay attention to this warning sign. These years were among the happiest of my life. An acquaintance I had known for more than ten years before I met Cain told me, I'm so excited for you! I've never seen you happier! I smiled and said, You're right, I've never been happier.

But there were a few things I should have paid closer attention to.

Once, Cain believed a local vendor had stolen money from him. He was upset, and I was sitting nearby as he spoke on the phone. The conversation escalated, and it was clear that Cain wouldn't get a refund. He blew a fuse. He started cursing and even threatened the vendor, saying, I can be down there in five minutes! How about I whip your ass when you leave? How about that, motherfucker?

I was shaken. I had never seen so much anger coming from Cain. The words made my stomach turn. It started feeling unsettled and painful. These sensations had served as my life-long indicators of needing to get away from the people who caused them.

Cain said, He hung up on me. I was looking at him with horror in my eyes while the pain in my stomach grew. All I wanted to do was leave. But he took my hand tenderly and kissed it and said, I'm sorry you had to witness that. His entire demeanor changed back to the considerate, kind, gentle, but strong man I knew. I asked why he'd gotten so upset and he said, I don't like people stealing from me, it really makes me mad.

I said that I understood and asked if he was really going to fight even hurt another person, over money.

I had learned long ago from a friend, Stanley was his name, that money is just energy and only has the power we give it. I saw money as paper I could use to purchase my needs and wants. It was how I provided for my family and community, that was all. I valued people more than money.

Cain replied, Well, when I said it, I meant it. But now, thinking about it, I'm not going to fight about it. Let's watch a movie.

My stomach had relaxed, and I reasoned Cain hadn't directed his anger at me, so I decided there was no reason to be anxious. Maybe this was just one of his emotional triggers— I didn't know what life experiences he'd had before we met. Someone must have stolen from him before, and this experience had brought back that memory. That was why he reacted so harshly. So, I only said, I like people to get along, and when they don't it really bothers me deep in my soul. He apologized again and said, Let me get something to drink. Then we can start the movie.

The second time, I had just gotten home from a long day at work. Cain was upset about an internal investigation at his job over an incident involving his wife and daughter that had taken place seven years earlier. He didn't go into detail, but he said he had disciplined his daughter, his ex-wife and his daughter later - called the authorities and filed charges against him, but later dropped them.

His work required security clearance, so any violation of the law was reported to his employer. He wasn't certain why this one had taken so long to show up, but he was very upset. He said, I will never speak with my daughter again. She is fucking with my job, my livelihood.

I was saddened to hear a parent say he would never speak to his child again for an offense like this.

I understood his being upset— who wouldn't be?— but to never speak with his child again seemed excessive. I said, Why not give the investigator their phone numbers? I'm sure once they speak, it can all be resolved easily. Instead, he picked up the phone, called his daughter, and went off on her. He told her that she dead to him and they would never speak again. My eyes were so wide I thought they'd get stuck that way.

Cain hung up and asked, Why should I have to deal with these people? They don't care about me, and I don't care about them.

I didn't advise him. I just left him alone, thinking he'd calm down and apologize to his daughter. In fact, it took almost a year before he would speak with her.

Then there was the time I locked the door between the garage and the laundry room. I was upstairs busy with something I don't remember, when I heard him calling my name. I went downstairs, and he went ballistic on me. He cursed at me and degraded me for locking the door. I was caught so off-guard that I just apologized. I told him, It's a habit I formed when you travel. I'm afraid of being in your house because I don't feel safe in your neighborhood. (He knew I had never lived in that part of town.) I'm sorry for locking you out, I said.

But while I was saying these words, my stomach went into over-drive. I was so jittery I could barely keep my balance. After I saw that he didn't care about my excuse, I left the room.

The next day, while I was alone, I received an email:

From: Cain
Sent: Tuesday, November 30, 2010 10:04 AM
To: Heart of the Deer
Subject: Question?

> Do you still love me or are you planning to leave? I didn't feel well yesterday.
>
> Cain

Here's how I replied:

From: Heart of the Deer
Sent: Tuesday, November 30, 2010 10:34 AM
To: Cain
Subject: Re: Question?

> What happened yesterday? Yes, I still love you. You should know I love you by my actions. After all, how else do we experience love, if not through the actions of others?

You need to understand that your actions are of great concern to me. What you did and what you said was of great concern to me. I like to know or be able to anticipate how the person I love will treat me. I don't want to walk on eggshells around you, and I don't want you to walk on eggshells around me. I don't want drama in my life. I don't want to fight and then make up. I don't like that kind of environment, and I reject anyone who embraces it.

I know that your childhood home wasn't always loving, and neither was mine. For people like us, it's important to break the cycle, because adults are still affected by their childhood experiences and can repeat the same behavior, or other behavior that yields the same impact in the end. That is, if they don't break the cycle. This is of great concern to me. I have worked hard to balance my experiences so that they have a positively effect on the people around me. I don't always succeed, but I work hard at it.

I know you are doing the same, but what happened yesterday yes this is of great concern to me.

Your actions yesterday reveal a truth. The question is, are we perceptive enough to comprehend it? What is the root cause? Is it your childhood? Is it that you prefer to live alone?

Was last night a clear sign that having someone in your home who does things differently upsets you? Is your need to control your environment stronger than your love for me? For that matter, could someone who truly loves me respond to me in such a shocking manner?

Yes, this is of great concern to me. Telling me you didn't feel well only shares an obvious and surface piece of the enigma, don't you agree? But please, my love, dig a little deeper. My challenge is to understand your actions without filling in the blanks. I need to allow you to be yourself. But who are you? Do I know you? What result did you hope to achieve, and why did you choose those actions to achieve it? Did you get the result you wanted? I want you to express yourself, but I want us to treat each other like we have been taught to treat those we love, because we have both been shown how to properly express love.

Yes, this is of great concern to me. I understand there will be times when I get on your nerves and times when your love for me is not the first thing you think of. At those times, I hope we can both treat each other with a principal love, the kind of love we show to strangers. We both deserve it, don't we? And if we can't display this love, shouldn't we ask ourselves why? If we can't, how many more yesterdays will we encounter? Where will we be, physically and emotionally, and how will we respond tomorrow? Yes, these things are of great concern to me.

I can't experience you today without reflecting on yesterday: on yesterday's love or lack of it, on yesterday's actions, desires, and intentions, and on the effect yesterday will have on tomorrow. Not to mention my personal responsibility to us— to you, to me, to our families, and to tomorrow. What really happened yesterday? Yes, this is of great concern to me.

I may not always write to express myself, but in my view of the world, love and actions go hand-in-hand. So please, my love, get a grip on today and tomorrow, because yesterday is gone. These are the things I thought about yesterday.

Sharing me,
Heart of the deer

Cain never replied to this or spoke about it. Instead he went back to being the wonderful man I had fallen in love with. I didn't want to create more confrontation, so I left the subject alone. I did contact my sister, though, and shared it with her.

My sister is the first friend I remember. I love her more than I have ever expressed, although I have tried. To know her is to love her. On the surface, she's strong, but there are tenderness and fragility under her persona. As my sister, her advice is always in my favor. She seems to assume I'm correct in my assessment of every situation, because she never asks questions that imply she is looking at it from all sides. I know that I had better not interrupt her while she's speaking. She always gives unedited, hard-core advice, which is usually over the top so I find myself not sharing much with her, but I do appreciate how hard she wants me to fight for myself.

After I shared this situation, she finished her assessment of it by saying, Tell that man to go kick rocks, you don't need him, and don't take any shit from him.

She said, Give him hell, fight back harder. I love you, and remember, you don't need him, he needs you.

I was encouraged by my sister's words and was happy I could turn to her for support.

I have a great ability to forgive, and when I do, it's as if the past never happened. With Cain returning to the person I'd fallen in love with, it was easy for me to forgive him. I never looked back on the situation that is until I wrote it here to share it with you. However, I should have seen his behavior as a warning, it would be my final warning. It was the most important one, because it was the one that was directed at me, but I disregarded it.

Six months later, we got married. I was happy. Cain's tribal leader gave us a book to read together. It had exercises that asked you to remember a time when this or that went wrong and think about how you could improve your response using the holy writing that was quoted. The problem was, I didn't remember the event that happened six months earlier. As far as I was concerned, we had never had a time when "this or that happened," so we couldn't do the exercises, and Cain lost interest in the process. Life with him was just so easy. Cain was my focus, the love of my life.

CHAPTER 4

AWAKENING

I have always been aware of light shining from the tops of peoples' heads. In the beginning, this light was dim, sometimes yellow and sometimes white, but I never paid attention to it. I never talked about it because I assumed that everyone saw it. It was like shadows: We see them around us all the time, but we don't usually talk about them. As an aside, thought, I believe shadows were created to mask the bleed-throughs that occur in the program.

When we go to sleep, we are actually reemerging into our real life. This is our true existence, where we have full knowledge. During this time, we have many experiences, but when we return to the holodeck, we pass through the waterfall of amnesia, which is a program for erasing our real life. During this process, we are sometimes inadvertently left with residual memories or experiences that emerge into our conscious minds afterward. That is one kind of bleed-through. Another happens as a result of other life forms visiting our planet. These life forms vibrate at different frequencies, and our equipment isn't advanced enough to detect them, so most people won't believe my words, but they are true. For those who start to awaken, interpretation of higher frequencies is a natural occurrence. Sometimes these energies appear as random shadows, and at other times the entire being is seen. These beings move about our planet just as we do. The ability to see what isn't easily perceived by the eye is called "clairvoyance," which just means to see clearly. I believe that by creating shadows of the physical, the programmer was masking potential bleed-throughs. We, the inhabitants, happily accept what we see and pay little attention to our sixth sense—that is, until we awaken.

It was Tommy who first brought up our sixth sense to me. We were at Oak Tree's house. She had invited everyone over to watch the Sunday night football game.

By this time, I had been welcomed into Cain's group of friends and felt right at home. I was sitting on the couch with my legs folded in an Indian position when Tommy said to me, When you are seated in that position, you maintain your power, but when you place your feet on the ground, you share your power.

It wasn't unusual for him to share his thoughts without us understanding him. But this time I said, Well, I like to share my power with the planet and all that is. And as the last syllable fell from my mouth, I placed my feet on the floor, and he just smiled. Then he said to Oak Tree, You were so pretty when you were younger. There were many men who wanted to be with you, but you were too picky. Now look at you. You are all alone, wanting someone to share your life with, but the years are starting to show and your options are much slimmer now. But know this: There is a white-haired man who has been watching you, and he is very interested in you. We will see if you can take advantage of this gift.

I didn't understand how he could just tell her what he did without worrying that it would hurt her feelings, but I was even more surprised by her reply. She didn't even acknowledge the first part of his statement. Instead she said, Well I don't think I know a man with white hair who's single.

Then Tommy said, He is around you, but you must pay attention.

She said, Ok, I will, but honestly, I can't think of a single person.

Then Tommy said with determination in his voice, He is there.

Next, Tommy turned to me and said, I know you see auras.

I didn't understand, so I frowned and said, What?

Then he said, Look at me and tell me what you see. So, I described his physical appearance, but he said, Not that. Everyone sees that. Tell me what you see that others cannot.

I said, Everyone in this room sees the same thing. We see you. Besides that, there is nothing.

Then he said it differently: I know you see colors. Look at me and tell me the colors you see.

But I said, Honestly, I just see you. The light above his head was not different from the light above everyone else's (except that his was pure white and very bright), and it never came to my mind to mention it. In all the years I'd been alive, I had never heard anyone talk about this light when describing a person.

But for the third time he said, I know you see colors around people. You don't have to be afraid to say it. I see them too. You and I have a lot in common.

Just then my husband chimed in, saying, Leave her alone, she said she doesn't see the colors. Tommy looked at him, and I heard Tommy's thoughts. He thought, I wasn't talking to you, but what he said was, You will never will see auras. You just don't know how lucky you are to have her, and you'll never be like us. With that, he turned and walked into the kitchen. Cain said to me, as he held my hand and kissed me gently on the forehead, don't listen to him. Sometimes he says crazy things.

I appreciated Cain standing up for me, but I didn't need him to. Tommy was our friend, and I wasn't offended. I was really trying to understand what he said. Tommy was passionate for sure, but he was passionate for sharing the truth, and I knew it.

I became preoccupied by the way I'd heard Tommy's private thoughts. I wondered what had made him change his words and why I hadn't heard those too before they came out of his mouth. I was puzzled. This was the first time I remembered hearing someone's thoughts.

Unfortunately, the easy life with Cain didn't last long. A few months after our marriage, I was permanently introduced to his other side. This was the one that challenged me, that rocked my foundation like an 9.5 earthquake, and it was he who caused my awakening. There are all sorts of reasons people awaken. My awakening happened because of extreme emotional pain.

I was almost ready for work when Cain asked me if I knew the weather forecast. I looked into his beautiful green eyes and said, 75 degrees and sunny. Then I smiled. That's when I saw something happen in his eyes. It was like the pupils grew in size so his eyes were now deep black. I didn't know what it meant, but before I could say another word he asked, Are you wearing that? you look horrible. I don't know why you spend so much time on your hair and makeup.

I took a deep breath and replied, Yes, I'm wearing this, and

I like the way it looks. Then I added, I've always taken the same amount of time getting ready. Then he went off on me. He started cursing at me and calling me names saying, You think you look nice, but you're wrong. You're chubby, you don't wear the right kind of clothes, you're totally irresponsible. He said I could never make up my mind about what I wanted, and that I was a drain on him. He said, I didn't know why the fuck I decided to get married again. He called me lazy and ugly and messy and said that he had been better off without me.

I felt the tears falling from my eyes and my sinuses overflowing. I hadn't seen this coming. He'd just asked about the weather. This time, instead of remaining cool, I yelled, Who do you think you're talking to? I'm not one of your kids. You may not speak to me like this! But my words started getting caught in my throat because I was crying and couldn't catch my breath.

I yelled, Did you call me chubby? I wear a size 6! I'm not chubby! And did you say I'm messy? Your home is cleaner than it was before I arrived. I'm a clean freak! What are you talking about? You're crazy! And as for irresponsible, I've worked a lifetime, and I have more responsibility and earn more than you. A drain on you? I'm the one who gives you money! You're totally crazy, I screamed through the tears that were now dripping from my lips.

Then I lowered my voice and asked in pain, How could you say these things to me? I don't know who you are, you're not the person I married. I'm not your property, and you can't talk to me like that.

He just started cursing more violently and threw something across the room. I thought he was going to hit me, but thank the Almighty he didn't. Instead he turned and walked out of the room, saying, You'd better have your ass home on time. I'm tired of waiting on you. A few minutes later I heard the garage door open and close, and he was gone.

When I got home from work, he was sitting in the family room, which I had to pass through to go upstairs. He knew I wouldn't speak with him because I hated arguing. So, as I walked past he just stared at me. It was horrible. I spent the rest of the night upstairs, but just before I fell asleep, he came into the room and sat on the bed. He said in a soft voice, You know I love you. I hate it when you yell at me. Let's not fight again. Then he kissed me on my forehead. It made my skin crawl. He said, I'm ok now, I forgive you.

I just laid there, not saying a word, but thinking, You are certifiably crazy.

The next five days were great. He was the man I fell in love with. He would cook me breakfast, lunch, and dinner. We went out to visit his friends so they could see how happy we were.

He treated me like he treasured me above everything. He made sure to hold my hand in public and kiss me whenever the chance arose, so that anyone watching would be envious of the love we shared.

We spent the ninth and tenth days at home. By this time he was starting to get irritable, and it increased until he exploded on the tenth day. And this was the cycle we fell into, every ten days.

Work was my escape, the place where I could be my happy self. I started scheduling business trips on the ninth and tenth days to avoid him, but I quickly learned that if he didn't have a tenth-day release, it would magnify in severity on whatever day I returned.

I know now that he never loved me. I just looked good on his arm, and that made him feel good, so that's where he wanted me. He tried to break me, to possess and dominate me, and for a time he did. I listened to him when he said, If you loved me you would accept all of me, and this is a part of me. I started asking myself if I'd done something to him that he was defending himself against. I started to lose my self-confidence. I got migraines that lasted days. For years, I listened to his attempts to convince me that I was the bad guy, that all couples fight sometimes, and that I was suffering from mental problems just because I expected couples to respect each other.

You may be wondering why I stayed. After all, he didn't hold me prisoner. I was free to go. The thing is, I had left my tribe and been excluded from my family, all with the hope of being free to make my own choices. I thought I had chosen someone good, and now it turned out he wasn't good to me. I was trying to understand how I had missed this side of his personality. After all, I had waited three years before I married him.

I thought that you certainly know a person after dating for three years, especially after living with them for one of those years.

I couldn't comprehend why he didn't see himself as the abuser. I wanted to understand what was happening so that I could help him and help us. I wanted to salvage the good things we had. I would fail at my second marriage if I didn't, and that was something I was determined to avoid. My ancestors taught me that if you don't learn life's lessons, you have to repeat them until you do. So, I stayed, determined to learn the lesson life was teaching me through this cruel teacher.

After months of dealing with this, I changed my focus from Cain to myself. I looked to my work as an escape and threw myself into it. I wanted to advance in my career, so I hired a life coach who exposed me to a new world. I learned about vibrations and energy. My ancestors had talked about vibrations and energy, but I hadn't fully understood. My life coach recommended books like *Excuse Me, Your Life is Waiting* by Lynn Grabhorn (it was the Acknowledgements section that was the key) and *Think and Grow Rich* by Napoleon Hill. I read everything I could get my hands on to find answers about my husband's behavior and to advance my career. I learned about family dramas. I learned about our sixth sense.

My awakening started to manifest itself in amazing ways, but I didn't know that I was awakening. My ability to hear what others were thinking increased, and the light I saw above people's heads changed. The colors started to stack into entire rainbows. During this stage, I received lots of pictures, like flash cards of events. I would see people's thoughts before they spoke them; sometimes the words never even came out of their mouths, because these were unconscious thoughts or just private ones.

I thought it was inconsiderate to listen to people's private thoughts, but I didn't know how to turn it off. Sometimes I would leave a party for the restroom and just place my hands over my ears and pray for the chatter to stop. It was too much stimulation. I also started channeling people's feelings. If they were happy, I'd feel happy, but if they were sad, I'd feel really sad. If people around me had done bad things, I would get sick. If I was in an elevator with someone who was involved in hurting our planet, people, or animals, I would hurt until I got away from them. I would always feel better when I was alone.

All of this was too much for me, so I asked Cain if we could do more things alone. He loved the idea and agreed. But many things kept happening. I could just think things, and they would happen. I could sometimes control Cain with just a thought but not consistently. I wanted to practice, but I didn't know how, because things were just happening that I couldn't find correlations between, or even triggers for them. I even went to a clan meeting hoping to find peace, but I didn't. I went to a doctor who tested me and concluded there was nothing wrong; I just had an over-active imagination. He just said that if it started taking over my life and I couldn't concentrate, he would consider seeing me again.

Then one day, Tommy said, You should call my friend. Here's her number. She's an old lady and very active in clan life. You have a lot in common with her, and she'll help you. The thing is, I hadn't told Tommy there was a problem. I conducted myself as I would normally, so none of our friends knew about my marital problems or the things I was hearing and seeing. I kept all of these things secret. So how did Tommy know I was going through a tough time? I took the card and told him, Thanks, maybe I'll call her. And later, I did.

She was a very sweet woman who shared many things to me. She said, My darling, you are not going crazy. You don't need a doctor, no, not at all, sweet girl. You have awoken. I can see your spiritual guides, and they have shared everything with me to assist you. But I'm not going to tell you much, because it will all fall into place for you very soon. You have many spiritual guides protecting and guiding you. That's how you found me. They sent you here. You are loved. You have a challenge with your husband, but that's for you to figure out. Let me know if you need anything. And let me thank you sincerely. It is a pleasure to have met and worked with you. You are truly blessed, and yours is a light that has been blessed by the Gods. I'm sometime saddened by the messages I have to share with people, but your story is one I'd happily retell. You are beautiful and loved. You are blessed, and so am I as a result of this exchange.

I thought, How could this be me? Blessed? I felt confused and frustrated because I didn't know how to manage all the pictures and words and emotions. I loved the words she said, but I didn't understand anything about spiritual guides and didn't know where to go for more answers. Then she said, as if reading my thoughts, You don't need any other teachers. You have the best ones with you. Watch and you'll see the truth of my words.

CHAPTER 5

AWAKE

I was working in my office when my attention was captured by a video that played in the air, above the guest seats. As I watched I saw myself sitting in my living room, and I was crying, it was a deep cry that made me think something terrible must have happened. When the video stopped, it disappeared as quickly as it appeared. I immediately picked up the telephone receiver and called everyone I could think of to make sure they were ok. After everyone confirmed all was well, I added I missed and loved them and hung up the receiver. I was left questioning the video that played, my thought was WTF, how could that happen and what does it mean? A few days later I lived out the vision. I had seen my future, but how could that be when the holy texts said there is no such thing as destiny? I was completely aware of the vision as the events unfolded and all I can say is – it was mind altering and shook me to my core. A whole new world with infinite possibilities opened to me. I began to learn truths that conflicted with my spiritual knowledge. Then one day, during a dinner party, the pieces of the puzzle started to come together.

I had gone outside to check on Tommy who was sitting on my porch surrounded by beautiful flowers. Water trickled and bubbled nearby, and a gentle breeze from the mountains was bringing a welcome break from the heat of the day. He was smoking a cigar, and every time he drew on it the ember at its tip glowed red-gold. When he exhaled, the scent of tobacco overtook the lavender in the air. In the distance, the early evening sky was painted in vibrant orange and red waves as the sun set. I'd wanted to make sure he had everything he needed, as I had been busy in the house with the other friends who had stopped by to unwind over a meal, drinks, and conversation at the end of a long week.

Tommy liked to smoke after he ate, and I asked that he indulge himself on the porch. Now I decided to sit beside him on the wicker chair. I liked hearing his views on many subjects, and he would share them freely as if someone had asked for them, even though no one ever did. He told me out of the blue, as if he were wishing me a good day, *You are a sensitive and you're awakening.*

With that, he began telling me things about myself, and things about my mother, my childhood, my past lives, and our friends who waited inside. I got goose pimples all over my body as he spoke, and I felt excitement and anticipation without knowing why. I was in shock, too. I didn't know how he knew these things, and my mind started racing with questions. But I pulled my focus back so I could process Tommy's words.

My first lucid thought was, How nice of you to say these things— you do know it all sounds crazy, don't you? But I couldn't deny the truths he shared. It was as if someone had given him every detail of my life since early childhood. I told him he was right about almost all of it, but not that I was "sensitive." I was not a sensitive person, I told him, and I gave him my reasons. Then he said, No, you misunderstand my use of the word, and he smiled this knowing smile. Like we do when we know something other people don't, and know that it's going to be cool to share it with them.

So, I asked what he meant by a sensitive, but he wouldn't

tell me. Instead he said, in the same matter-of-fact tone, while puffing again on the cigar, Look it up— but don't use the dictionary. Go to YouTube. Remember, he said, *You are a sensitive*, and a powerful one— on a scale of one to ten, you're a nine, he said. And he added that he was envious because he knew I wouldn't want anything all to do with my "gift"— that I would be afraid of it.

He said, I wouldn't share this with you, but you're an old soul and you've been working at this for a long time.

So, he went on, telling me about all the glorious lives I'd lived. I listened with my eyes wide, thinking he must be confused. Did he say *past lives?* I didn't believe in reincarnation. I thought maybe he was thinking of someone else, but he kept looking at me, his eyes full of conviction, determined to convey his message. And as if he was reading my thoughts he said, I'm not confused. Listen to what I'm telling you. This is all about you. You've lived glorious lives and you owe it to yourself and all that is to give back in this life. I've wanted to tell you this from the first time we met, but the time was never right. Then he said, It's an honor to know you.

As he spoke those words I looked around to see if anyone else was on the porch, then I turned back and said, I don't understand. His final words were, You will understand. Oh yes, you will.

Tommy had been a family friend for years. For that matter, we'd known most of our friends for a long time, and all of them were believers. No one talked about past lives, or even thought about them as far as I knew. That stuff was foreign to most of them. Tommy who had three master's degrees and was almost finished his PhD— was the only one who spoke of magical things. He was in his forties, he served in the armed forces, and he'd traveled to many countries. He was experienced, and he was someone I respected.

At the time, I think anyone overhearing Tommy's kind words might have thought he was making a pass at me, but he wasn't. He was sincere. There was power and conviction in his words so strong I could feel it. I didn't ask, because I didn't want to insult him, but I did wonder, Are you really directing me to go to *YouTube* for a definition?

And I mentally started to shake my head. Not my idea of an authority on definitions. And did you say, I'm an old soul? I wouldn't have described myself that way. Actually, I thought I had a young soul.

What Tommy didn't know is that I had been experiencing many strange things. I didn't discuss them with him because I sensed that his logic interfered with his ability to comprehend and that his lens was very different from mine.

After everyone left, my mind returned to Tommy's words. *You are a sensitive.* I searched YouTube for "What is a sensitive?" A lot of videos popped up, showing freeze-frames of many different people. I don't trust things on the internet too quickly, and I'm careful before I visit sites. I searched the faces for one that looked honest, happy, good— someone who seemed to be in a desirable environment both mental and physically. How I could know *that* just by looking at a picture, I can't explain. I just knew I would. I've always relied on my gut instinct. It's my most trusted companion, and this night I used my faith in this heavenly gift to navigate the site.

I scrolled down, and that's when I saw Heidi Sawyer. She sat in front of a draped window, next to a small table. Her eyes seemed kind and wise; on the table was a colorful sculpture of an elephant. I looked at her face, it seemed normal; nothing really stood out about it. I loved the red, gray, and blue that decorated the room. All these things felt good, so I clicked on her link, and the video began.

Heidi spoke with an English accent that made the whole experience seem light. Despite that, she was very serious as she explained what a sensitive person was. It was like having a kindergarten teacher explain to you that one and one make two.

I was shaken when she casually remarked, If you're still viewing this video, you are a sensitive; you would have lost interest by now if you weren't.

And yet when she said that a sensitive person is a psychic, my mind shouted, No, not a psychic! No, no, that's bad, it's wrong! And then I remembered Tommy's words. At once I understood why he was smiling and why he said I wouldn't want anything to do with "the gift" because of he knew how I loved the Holy text. My mind flooded with all the passages that mentioned psychics, and I thought, No, Tommy, no way . . .

But in the back of my mind and in my body, something else was going on. I felt excitement deep within, and I heard myself think, so that's what's happening to me. The excitement grew. I scolded myself for my thoughts. I told myself, Okay, this is enough now, stop, turn off the computer, this is rubbish! The thing is, I didn't want to stop listening to Heidi. What she said made sense and resonated deeply with me. So, I didn't stop. I listened more, and at Heidi's encouragement I visited her website. I wanted to hear more. She had a free book there called *I Know You Better Than You Know Yourself.* You must be thinking, Boy are you gullible, and on some subjects, I might be, but not when it comes to knowing myself, my beliefs, and the world I live in. My beliefs are strong, and I know the Holy Texts better than most people. I've studied them for decades. Because of my strong faith, I wasn't worried about downloading the book. I read Heidi's story. I looked further, to see if she was credible, and found that many people love her and look to her for an understanding of what it's like to be a sensitive in our society.

From the beginning, Heidi's words soothed me. They just felt good. She explained the difference between a sensitive and a non-sensitive.

She described an extra-sensitive nervous system. As an example, she spoke about the animal kingdom. In packs of animals, there are always a few that can sense hidden dangers. These ones move, and the herd follows. The first animals to move are sensitive to their environment. They sense hidden energies that they interpret as dangers, and they signal to the herd that it's time to move on. Those who move live another day. Those who don't might end up as prey. And the same thing is true of humans, Heidi said. Some of us can intuitively sense the unseen things— or, to put it better, unseen energies.

Heidi spoke of sensitives having unsettled feeling in their

stomachs. My own stomach had been overactive my whole life, but I'd just assumed everyone had the same problem. It made me feel jittery and nervous most of the time. I couldn't remember a time that it wasn't sending me signals. It would say, This is a friend, a foe, danger, excitement, without ever being asked, and I couldn't turn it off. In order to function, I learned to breathe deeply and change my focus. No one ever told me to do this. It was just what I did, and it helped. I called my gut feeling a trusted companion, as I've said. That's because I learned to understand the signals it sent me.

I'm sure you've had the feeling of butterflies in your stomach at times in your life, or the sudden sensation of your stomach turning over. If you recall those sensations and multiply them, you'll have an idea of how I felt most of the time. And no, I don't have a medical condition. I'm fit, I have a low BMI. I'm in excellent health. But my sensations would always demand my attention. They ranged from a low nervous hint to a hyper-intense feeling that sometimes even hurt. They would grow stronger and louder until I listened to them and acted. That's how I learned to use them when I made decisions.

Heidi was the first person I heard discuss these feelings and explain where they came from. She said that we live in a vibrational environment, with energy all around us, and sensitives perceive this energy. There was no hocus pocus, just energy. I remembered that my ancestors had talked about energy and vibration too, so I was comfortable with the example. Heidi said these feelings are natural and we need to learn to relax with them. She offered a free relaxation meditation, so I tried it to see if it would help. And it did. Not only was I relaxed, but I felt solid. The jittery feeling that had been my life-long companion drifted away, replaced by a grounded, stable feeling that I really liked. That doesn't mean the sensations never return, but now I know why they arise and how to manage them. All I can say is, Thank you, Heidi!

Heidi also shared her life story and told how she'd learned these truths. She described the opening signs of being a psychic. The crazy thing was, most of the things she mentioned happened regularly to me.

From that day forward, I looked to Heidi for information. This was all new to me, and I intuitively trusted this lady to guide me. After all, she'd helped me get rid of my jittery stomach, which I'd never thought possible. I bought books and other products and found them informative and helpful. I was fascinated because the things she said made sense and were easy to understand. She took a subject that I had feared and avoided, and laid it out plainly. She removed the veil of mystery and relieved my anxiety.

The people these things happened to, she explained, were sensitives, and this isn't something you can avoid. She even described things that had happened to her to show why you shouldn't avoid the warning signs.

Those signs can be small, but they can increase in severity until you are forced to acknowledge who you are. She said that sensitives were psychics, mediums, or channels, which didn't appeal to me at all. I'd been taught to avoid those practices because my family believed they were evil and that the Almighty didn't approve of them.

But Heidi likened the sensitivity that I and others had to kind of a guidance system, like a car's oil gage. When the gage turns red, it's a signal that you need to change the oil. If you don't pay attention to your figurative oil gage, your situation won't improve. It gets worse until your engine fails. That's what happens to sensitive people who ignore their guidance Heidi said.

Heidi encouraged her listeners to make their own decisions. As for me, meditation helped me refuel, figuratively, so I started doing it daily. But I asked myself, How does this stranger know so much about me? And why should I believe someone I don't even know? What if she has an agenda? What if she's trying to trick people into moving into her world? I wondered how I could turn my back on decades of teachings that opposed what this stranger taught.

These questions remained a part of my internal chatter for years, because I wanted to be sure I was doing the right thing. What I decided was that my own life experiences offered me evidence, so I would test what I was learning against them. I remembered our most famous prophet's words: A rotten tree cannot produce good fruit, you will know it by its fruit. I know that evil results in things that a good person doesn't want, and that doing good results in good things, things desired. I had practiced Heidi's meditation, and the result was a strong, solid, balanced, and grounded feeling in my body. I believed this to be good. So I continued my studies.

I'm a person who should be led by my gut feelings. I didn't need Heidi to recommend that, because I'd always done it. So, I decided to use my internal guidance system to decide whether to move forward and learn from this woman. I prayed that my instincts would remain alert and warn me before I got too deep into a situation to find my way out.

I also know that our creator is the most powerful being there is and can read my heart. He knew that I didn't want to be disobedient, but simply to grow and fully live the life he had blessed me with. I knew he would rescue me if I was being deceived, and I prayed to him for his guidance.

I decided I would consider Heidi's ideas and compare them with my own knowledge, experience, and feelings. I would keep them if I believed them and reject them if I didn't. I felt I would be able to weed things out myself. Some people learn the easy way, by reading, observing, or being taught. Others must learn through personal experience. Sometimes personal experience is hard: many things happen on our planet that we wouldn't want to experience personally. I've learned by all these methods, and this time I decided I would try to learn the easy way.

Although I didn't believe that psychics were good in the Almighty's eyes, I reasoned that I wouldn't be psychic if the Almighty hadn't made me that way. I reasoned my ability to hear the thoughts others had and to feel their feeling, which lots of people have was natural after all I didn't do something to make it happen it just happened. I saw auras around people too— colors stacked over and around their bodies— and I always see things out of the corner of my eye like shadows, but I had always thought these were optical illusions that everyone encountered. When the phone rang, I knew who it was before I answered, or I knew the phone would ring before it did.

I'd know a person from a picture or by holding an object and seeing a video of their life in my mind. But all these things I lumped together as coincidences or an over-active imagination, and I didn't share them with anyone. Now I knew that this was a normal process, and I should trust the things I learned, as they would help me and others in my life.

Heidi also said it was important to know what kind of "clair" you were. I didn't know what a clair was. She explained that sensitive people are clairvoyant, clairaudient, or clairsentient— it's how you receive your psychic ability. Most people, she said, start out clairsentient— having feelings in your stomach. Yikes, I thought, that was true for me. For some people, though, that was only the beginning, and their true clair nature would become predominant later on. She said this physic development would happen naturally for some.

I wanted to read as much as I could about the amazing things that were happening to me. I wanted to find other people who had experienced the same things to be sure I wasn't going crazy. Then there was the life coach I hired who was helping me professionally, and things began flowing amazing easily into my life. It was like I was high on life, and I loved the sensation. Anytime I thought about a book, or someone told me about one, another person would give me that very book or I'd run into it without even looking for it. I began receiving clearer information. I knew in advance the things I needed to do. And if I wanted something to happen, I just had to think of it and it would happen like magic. My ancestors say there is no such thing as a coincidence, really— that everything that happens has a meaning, and it's just up to us to pay attention if we want to master navigating through life. Now my life experiences had me focused on their advice.

It interested me the way people can experience the same thing but see the experience very differently. I wanted to know why this was, so I started reading anything I could get my hands on, and I came across a name I'd seen two months earlier. That name was Abraham Hicks. The first time I saw his name was in the author's acknowledgements in *Excuse Me, Your Life Is Waiting* by Lynn Grabhorn. I'd had made a mental note to look him up, but I hadn't followed through. Months later, I was reading about the law of attraction. I learned that Esther Hicks was the mother of the law of attraction, so I made another note to look up her. Hold on to your britches— what I found was even weirder than grasping that I was a sensitive. Esther Hicks was Abraham Hicks. I did a double take at that. I said to myself, Slow down, reread, and focus. It turned out there was a woman named Esther Hicks (happily married, mother, and productive citizen who was teaching the law of vibration, attraction, and allowing by channeling her spiritual guide, Abraham.

Say what?

I read that Esther had been happily living with her second husband. So, I found a picture of Esther Hicks on the computer, and I studied her face. Her eyes were small and brown, and something about them just seemed kind. But it was her voice that really struck me. When I heard it, I felt immediate trust. I detected sincerity, honesty, and joy— things I would not call evil. I remembered again our most famous prophet's words that a bad tree cannot produce good fruit. This woman felt good and was producing good fruit. People all over the world were giving testimony to that fact.

I listened to her husband too. He explained that Esther was like a translator. She received information that she framed in English words. In Esther's husband, too, I perceived excitement, exuberance, and intelligence.

Her husband was easy to listen to, and I got caught up in his liveliness. It was Esther's voice, though, that soothed me. Her words gave me comfort, and the things she said resonated with me, and I believed her.

Many of the things she said were part of my core beliefs already. I knew, for example, that life was meant to be joyous, and no one could ever convince me otherwise, even though not all my experiences had been joyous. People have tried to convince me that life is hard, that it's all about hard work, and that people can't be trusted because they're selfish and want things from you. I've been told to be on guard and not to trust people.

Of course, I believe in working for what you want. I knew that life is full of challenges, and that sometimes it's like a puzzle you can't solve. And I knew there were evil people in our world who took advantage of the kind people. But I also knew that life is meant to be fun. I've always known that, just like I know that it's okay to go to sleep each night because I'd wake up each morning. Life is meant to be joyous, and people, although sometimes we get off track, are good, and there is much more good than evil in the world. I believe that being good or evil is a decision, so most of the time I decided to be kind and positive and know that things would work out. No one could ever convince me that all men cheat or that everyone is selfish all the time. I knew no person was more blessed than another, and that the Almighty's doesn't play favorites. We are all equal.

We have differences, different gifts, of course, but each of us has been given what we truly need. Each of us have the same opportunities to use the laws of this planet to create the lives we want to live.

I can't help recalling the image of Tommy sitting on my front porch, it's like that was where he was supposed to work, on a porch, telling people things about themselves to help them remember or awaken. That night, my life changed. Yes, Tommy was correct I am a sensitive. The funny thing is, you are too.

CHAPTER 6

THERE IS NO PART OF MY DNA THAT WAS PROGRAMED TO BE SMALL: PRESENT DAY

Four and a half years later, what do I believe? I believe that this planet is very different from what most people think, can I prove this, no, but I don't need to because I'm not trying to convince you of anything. I'm simply sharing the unfolding of my life. I believe people are capable of much more than we accept as true and my experiences provide testimony of this truth. In chapter one, I shared one of the clues that will lead to the path of knowledge, but there are many others. If you pay attention, you will find them in nursery rhymes, stories, songs, movies, and legends. They have been placed in plain sight, firmly established for current and future generations to discover.

Those who identify the clues are immediately documented by the Cosmos. Their names and locations are transferred to earthly ambassadors who manage secret societies that guard knowledge and tradition. Once these guardians have a person's name, they begin an investigation into the person. If you are recognized as someone who will contribute to all that is in an important way, they will reach out to you, it's not the other way around. The invitation will be tempting but know membership requires a lifelong commitment. You cannot leave, so be certain before you join. If you join, you will have access to vast knowledge. The education program is unmatched in our civilization and usually appeals to seekers because the quest for knowledge is what fuels them. It's unfortunate that most of these people never qualify for membership. I'm not advocating or discouraging membership in the societies. I want everyone to know they exist because they are part of our heritage.

If you accept the invitation, your life will change, but the change won't be obvious to the ones who are asleep. Humility, love, and service are important to develop. But because membership is exclusive, you will risk becoming an elitist, rejecting others who have awakened but don't qualify for membership. You will do well if you understand membership is not essential for becoming fully awake and proficient in the mastery of life on this planet. The Cosmos is free to share with whomever it deems worthy. Many awakened ones possess powers that defy our normal understanding of physics.

Some are even more powerful than the masters in these societies.

There are many awakened ones who have no knowledge of these secret societies because they have not qualified for membership. These people will do well as long as they understand that their ignorance of the secret societies does not absolve them of responsibility. Part of that responsibility involves respecting others and where they stand in the process. Another part has to do with anonymity: no one should use their gifts in public, as this could disturb the natural processes of the sleeping ones and bring unsuitable attention.

Regardless of which group we fall into, we must respect the knowledge we have been blessed with and continue our growth and contribution to the program.

To those of you who are asleep: please know the energy of our planet has changed and more than likely you will be faced with realities that force you to awaken in the near future. When it arrives, know there are light bears ready to assist and easy the process. The sooner you accept that we are not alone, the less traumatic the process will be.

There are many beings from other dimensions who watch us. They document our lives; nothing is done in secret on this planet. All our actions have consequences, so be observant and careful as you navigate.

Those of you who believe you are alone and that these words are part of a fantasy: It is you who are in the deepest sleep. Enjoy your slumber because soon you will awaken. You have been put on notice.

The awakening process is different for each of us, but you can do some things to manage it, and these are universal.

First, accept there are no coincidences in life. This planet is alive and sends insects, animals, people, and events to convey messages. It is our responsibility to interpret these messages and decide how to react. As you navigate, remember: Love is the most powerful weapon. Treat yourself and all others including our precious planet, with love. Love is healing, and you will find that it benefits you most of all.

This program, this classroom or holodeck, is fragile. There are many lower energies seeking domination, which could result in total collapse. Balance is necessary for efficient, productive, and healthy existence. I won't invest any more words in these lower energies, as my whole- souled desire is for them to be freed and gently reunited with love— after all, any of us can lose our way. It is not part of our role to judge energy. We evaluate energy and state our preferences through our actions; that is all.

Let the light of love be your guide. Pay attention to the road, as it is narrow and has many branches. Sometimes finding the way to go is difficult, so always look for love's light. Sometimes it's dark and there's no clear sign of love's light; at these times, be still, meditate, and wait. Love's light will soon shine to provide you with clear direction.

Move forward when you are certain, and don't beat yourself up if you stray off course. Sometimes that's part of your development. Remember, we should learn from all our experiences. Love's light will still be there, and all you need to do is call to it and be patient. It will reply by guiding you back on course.

I'm often told the purpose of life is to take care of your family, to support and guide them, and to contribute to society. I agree that these are among our responsibilities, but there is more.

Don't short-sell yourself or your family; commit to growth. But if growth isn't your desire, I honor that too. I just want people who desire freedom and self-expression to break free of the subjugation we underwent as we grew. I mean "break free" like a butterfly breaks free of its cocoon.

We have a responsibility to find our gifts and use them for the benefit of everything that is. It takes determination to think differently from your programing, but you will only live your most fulfilled life when you decide to be uniquely yourself. The subjugation process has stifled too many for far too long. You are beautiful. Don't be afraid to show the world who you are and what you prefer.

It's sad that most of us are so enchanted by the life we are living that we disregard anything outside of what we currently perceive. But I know there are people like you and me who are searching for answers, and it is to these people that I speak.

I have shared a few of my life lessons as testimony that everything works out in the end— at least if you slow down, pay attention, create the life you want by using your psychology, and embrace love's light. I wrote this to ease the awakening process for others and to let them know they aren't alone. You're not going mad or insane. Your gifts may be manifesting, which can be unnerving, but there is help. Sheila and Marcus Gillette and Heidi Sawyer have made it their lives' focus to remove the veil of superstition and explain logically what is happening during the awaking process. They have been vital to me. Heidi was my first teacher, and her relaxation meditation was a pivotal experience. Although she might not agree with everything I've written, she is willing to assist those who are awakening to their gifts.

Years later the teachers Sheila and Marcus Gillette came into my life. Sheila is a direct voice channel for Theo. Theo is a collective of 12 Archangels that are mentors and teachers. Through their work, I have experienced and witnessed the most beautiful healings, done with gentleness and love. They have a soul integration course that provided me with tools to release past trauma. They too may not agree with all that I have written, but if you're looking for teachers, I highly recommend them. You can visit their website asktheo.com to learn more.

For full disclosure, I must tell you that I know and love this couple.

As I grew, my needs changed, so new teachers came.

The main ones are affectionately called My Esther.

There are many other teachers out there. By their fruits, you will know if they are right for you. Remember, the Cosmos is watching, and it is willing to send you assistance, but you must ask for it. Just ask, and your request will be heard. Do all things in love, and love will reply. Trust that your answers are coming, and watch to see how miraculously they manifest.

You can find love's light throughout the process. Just look for it.

AFTERWORD

I moved out of Cain's house in August 2013. For the next 18 months, I saw him on weekends to give us space and time to work through our challenges. But it saddens me to say, we couldn't grow together. I divorced him in July 2015, though he pleaded with me outside the courtroom. These will be my final words to him:

> *You have tried to discredit my intellectual competence, but I forgive you. I know that your battle isn't with me but with yourself, a fierce warrior. You are in pain, and to assuage it you lash out at me, but it doesn't work. The laws of our planet mirror behavior and psychology back on the person who generates them. So, it is upon yourself that you inflict pain. I'm so sorry for that, but really, could there be a better justice system?*
>
> *During our marriage, you abused me and took advantage of my love for you. But your mind games, manipulation, control, and denigration have backfired because your dark shadow energy is not strong enough to dim my light of love. I will always love you, but I say no to abuse. When I left you, I was finding the strength to finally stand up for myself. It was an act of self-love, which I celebrate and recommend. I gave you many chances before I left, because you promised you had changed, but every time your abuse escalated and I learned that nothing had changed.*

Although you had every right to conduct yourself as you pleased, you did not have the right to possess and dominate me. So, I executed my own right to remove myself from your association. Now you are trying to make me out to be the bad guy, but all along it was you who acted irrationally and perpetrated abuse.

You know this and so does God, the Cosmos, or whomever you deem the supreme being. This one bore witness to my treatment and will testify on my behalf. I pray that you acknowledge it and seek forgiveness before you make the final transition through death. I know it will be far easier on you if you do this while you are in physical form.

You may be surprised to hear that, after all you put me through, my love for you has not wavered. I will always be here for you if you need me. I take the same position I did before our divorce: I see you clearly, all of you: the good and the fear. I want to focus on the good. This is because I believe in the power love has to transform people. I believe in the synergy of thought. Maybe my thoughts of you conducting yourself in love will give you the energy you need to break free of your fears. But whatever the result, I know that love never fails, so I will continue to extend love toward you.

I will forever be grateful to you for the lessons you taught me. The first was self-respect. I finally learned to stand up for myself and tell the world through my actions that I matter and that the way people treat me matters. The second was how to finally look at the abuse I suffered as a child, how to thank it and release it. Now I'm free from the abuse and invisible to abusive people. My only regret is that it was you who were so willing to teach me this lesson and that I had to learn it through abuse.

Twenty-six months later, I'm single and enjoying the peace, health, and prosperity that are byproducts of being awake.

I have learned from the people I mentioned, but I've had other teachers too, more than I can list. I'm still learning and evolving.

But my most important truths come from within. I trust me. I know me, and I will continue to learn the lessons of my life, share, and grow, never holding to just one road.

I've shared the unfolding of my own truths with you. Yours might unfold very differently. Just know that you owe it to yourself to grow. Of course, if you elect not to, that's your right too.

And as a closing thought, I would like to say this: Everyone has some psychic ability. Heidi compared it to running. Some of us are star runners, some of us do it for fun, and some of us don't want to run. The point is, we have more in common than not.

THE END

REFERENCES

ELIPHELET Oram Lyte, Row, row, row your boat nursery rhyme

Writer? Be careful what you wish for you just might get it

Abraham Hicks, Esther Hick, Jerry Hicks

Napoleon Hill, *Think and Grow Rich*

Lynn Grabhorn, *Excuse Me Your Life Is Waiting*

Marcus and Sheila Gillette, *Theo*

Heidi Sawyer

My Esther